Rising Strong

How I Became A Soldier For Recovery

Suleiman Hassan

Copyright © 2024 by Suleiman Hassan

All rights reserved. This book or any portion thereof may not be reproduced or used in any manner whatsoever without the express written permission of the publisher, except for the use of brief quotations in a book review.

Printed in the United States of America

For more information please visit:

www.soldiersforrecovery.com

Dedication:

First, I want to say thank you to God, for everything he has done on his journey of life. I would like to thank my mother, I would like to thank my wife for being such a supportive woman and a backbone. I wouldn't be able to do what I'm doing for the world if it wasn't for my wife. I would like to thank my children, my three beautiful children, as well as my grandson. I would like to thank my family that I didn't mention, and friends that I didn't mention, and everyone who supported me along this journey to get **"Soldiers for Recovery"**, where it is today, and where it's going.

Tables of Contents

Dedication

Introduction

Chapter 1: The Cause

Chapter 2: The Transition

Chapter 3: The Pain

Chapter 4: Surrender

Self Help & Resources

Conclusion

About the Author

Become a Soldier for Recovery

Introduction:

The Life of Suleiman Hassan, founder of *"Soldiers for Recovery"* began in 1979. The year he was born to his mother, Glenda Oliver and his father, Ali Hassan. Suleiman Hassan grew up in a large family with six siblings, no sorry, nine siblings. He has six sisters, and two brothers on his mom's side, his dad's side consists of 21 more kids. Growing up in West Philly wasn't always peaches and cream, because due to his mom and father, separating when he was six years old, led to a dark, dark life. Because during this separation, his mother got introduced to drugs and alcohol. And as Suleiman Hassan continued to grow up his responsibility of helping to raise his brothers and sisters became rough for him and his older brother. In this story, you will find how Suleiman Hassan was able to beat the odds. But he had to go through so much pain, so much trauma, and what you will learn later on in the book, some of his experiences, and what he is doing today to stay sober, as well as save lives from the disease of addiction.

Chapter 1:

Suleiman Hassan grew up in West Philadelphia, in a very large family. And his home has eight siblings, a loving mother, and a loving father. His mother was very hands on with him and all the children. And to this day, I still don't understand how she managed to do that, but she did it very well. We had birthdays, we had breakfast, lunch, and dinner. Of course, school was a big part of our home. And my mother even took the time to teach us how to plant flowers, taught us songs we sang, we danced, every day was something different, especially in the summer. In summertime, when she would allow us to go out front or go in the backyard. And we will have lots of fun doing the same things that I just mentioned. But at the same time, there were a lot of days that my mom was often sad. And this is during the time that we were even living with my father. I didn't know what was really happening or going on. But she was able to manage herself in a way that we wouldn't know she was being abused. On top of that in the early 80s, we were the only Muslim family in West Philadelphia at the time. I know you may find that hard to believe but it's true.

So a lot of times my mother stayed covered so we couldn't see what was going on beyond her eyes.

Eventually, I've come to learn later on in my adult years that my father was addicted to heroin and alcohol. And during those childhood years my father would come home and beat my mother. And that's why a lot of times she would have a face cover because she was marked up with bruises from my father beating her. Eventually my mom got tired of the abuse and came to my brother and I to say we had to leave the house, we didn't know what was going on. I was about six years old at this time. All I can remember is my mom waking us up and rushing us through the backyard. We had to climb over the fence. And all I remember was dogs barking, me being scared, me being confused, and crying because I didn't really know what was going on. So we wound up going to the police station, and my mother set my brother and I down and told us to wait. She went in there and talked to the police. Then after that, the cops came, talk to my mother and then we wound up going back to the house and her getting the rest of my brothers and sisters out of the house. And once that happened, we wound up living in the shelter. So now I am only six years old, and I've encountered my first experience of dealing with trauma. Coming from a home where my mom was always a provider for her family to now having the shelter providing for us was a traumatizing experience to witness.. Someone else telling us when to use the bathroom was very uncomfortable for me. And all I could think about was what's my father, where is my dad? I remember this song from Michael Jackson called "Human Nature". This was a song by Michael Jackson that I used to listen to as a child when I was living in the shelter, surrounded by nothing but strangers. And to this day, it brings tears to my eyes, because it makes me sad to listen to. So after a while of living in the shelter, we were there for about six to nine months. My mother wound up getting a house, a big house. The house was beautiful. It was about seven bedrooms in Southwest Philly. My mother let us go outside. My mother would keep my sisters in the house. And at this time we started experiencing being outside without staying in the backyard or the front porch. One day, it was this guy dressed in the army suit, he came to the house. And us being curious kids, we looked out the window because this man was dressed, he was dressed up very nice. And we were curious about who he was.

Eventually, he wound up coming into our house and he started coming over more. After several more visits we'd come to find out it was my mom's boyfriend. This was after three years of her being alone. And now that I'm older, I understand that everyone needs someone. But at that time, as a child, I was seven years old when this happened. Eventually, we moved from Southwest Philly from a seven bedroom house to a four bedroom house. Imagine, my mother at that time she had eight of us and eventually gave birth to my little sister, but that's later on down the line. But we moved into this very small house in West Philadelphia across the street from the supermarket. My mother went from making breakfast, lunch and dinner to just breakfast and lunch. Then from breakfast and lunch to just lunch, and eventually to nothing. We didn't know what was going on. Some days, I didn't even see my mother, but came to find out her boyfriend introduced her to crack cocaine. This was in 1986. Eventually, during that time, we didn't have any rules. All the rules and the structure left when we moved into this tiny house. We ran the streets, me and my brother. Some days we didn't come home until one or two in the morning, a lot of times we didn't have anything to eat. And thank God for the supermarket across the street because they would come and deliver the food and they knew it was a family with nine kids living across the street with a mother who was addicted to drugs and alcohol. What I'm talking about is trauma. A lot of days I went to sleep with nothing, a lot of days I cried. Because at the same time me and my brothers and sisters were the ones who were getting bullied. We were the ones who went to school hungry. We were the ones that got chased. We were the ones that, you know, had to survive some kind of way. So those days were very, very painful for me.

I remember having to go in the dumpster for food across the street behind the supermarket. Because some days we didn't have any food at all. But we knew it was some bread or something we could eat inside the dumpster across the street. The first of the month, my mom will get food stamps. And she will go food shopping for us. And just for that one day, we have food, maybe two, the most of us. Those were some of the best days, the first of the month when the food stamps came, because we knew at least for a couple of days we're going to have something to eat. Before waking up during that same week, we will have a freezer, refrigerator full of food to waken up just nothing because due to my own mother, and her boyfriend at the time struggling with their disease of addiction, they eventually sell everything. I remember getting sneakers and clothes that my mother would give us to go to school, and the next day our clothes and sneakers will be sold for drugs. I'm very young, so I didn't understand anything but pain and it was very painful for me growing up. So eventually I wound up hanging out with other kids that were going through the same thing that I went through, which inevitably led me to a life of crime.

Chapter 2:

So eventually, I started hanging out with people who were just like me, other young individuals, all juveniles that ran the streets, who had no curfews, who had no fathers in their homes, and mothers who were on crack. So we all did the same things. We hung out, we used to start pumping gas at gas stations, just to put money in our pocket to buy us something to eat. I would use my money to take home to my little sisters to make sure they eat. And sometimes help out mom with a bill here and there. Eventually, I've learned how to make my way into selling drugs myself. In my mind, I had to survive. And at the same time, it wasn't a ruse. So, me and my friends, on top of us taking packs from the neighboring drug dealers or people who run the neighborhood. We all got together and we started selling our own drugs. And once drugs got on the table, our lives became unmanageable. And I'm talking about age 12 or 13. While selling drugs I was introduced to smoking weed. And then I got introduced to stealing cars.

Back in the day, you could take a car down North Philly all day long, and sell it to whoever you're gonna sell it to. And they'll pay you about $300, $400 for each car you bring. So on top of being addicted to a hustler lifestyle I also got addicted to weed, stealing cars and then selling them. It was a rush for me. My friends and I always had an inventory of cars, which were all stolen. We always had weed to smoke, and we always had some money because we were selling drugs as well. Not knowing that I'm falling into a slippery slope as well as getting used to addictive lifestyle behavior, which seemed normal.. See, no one told me that life would be like this. No one told me later on that I will become an addict. But I kept spiraling out of control at such a young age. Deep down inside, I was still hurting because of how I was brought up. The lack of love and attention from both of my parents due to substance abuse, led me to feel alone most of the time even though I had several brothers and sisters. It was still something deep inside of me that kept hurting and was too young to understand what it was. Now that I'm older and sober I now know deep down inside it was love.

Eventually, I wound up getting arrested for stealing cars and ended up serving three and a half years of my life in juvenile prison between the ages of 14-17. In jail, I did have a few moments of clarity, but I went through a lot of difficulties in there as well. Believe it or not they also had drugs inside of jail, as well as groups from different parts of Pennsylvania. I'm from Philly, so that's who I rolled with. So when I went in there, it wasn't hard to find people who were just like me. Truth be told, everybody in there was just like me anyway regardless of where they came from, because most of us, we just needed love. So by the time I came home, I was two weeks away from my 18th birthday. When I got released I came home to a daughter that was birthed while I was still imprisoned. Two weeks from 18 to a brand new daughter that I had to father and take care of. At first I was on track. Got me a job. I dropped out of high school because I had to take care of her. I wasn't drinking, I wasn't smoking, but eventually due to me and her mother separating, it caused me to go back out to sell drugs, and eventually drinking again, and smoking again. During this time, I started moving about a kilo a month, and eventually to about a kilo every two weeks. Selling drugs became very addictive. I wound up picking up drinking more and more not realizing that I became an addict myself. I was addicted to the money, the cars, the women and I thought everything was fine. But then one day I found out the daughter that I was fathering wasn't mine which led me into depression. So at the age of 21, I found out a daughter wasn't mine that I father from the age of 17. So that was four years of me fathering a child. And it felt like my world was snatched away from me, which led me into deep depression. And I found myself drinking all day and all night just to cope with the pain.

But when I got sober I realized that I wasn't just drinking for those reasons. I was also drinking because of my upbringing. Eventually I wound up meeting my wife at the age of 21. When I laid eyes on her, I knew that she was the one. I knew that she'll be the one that sticks with me through rain, sleet, hail, snow, or whatever that I will go through in life. My wife accepted me and my biological daughter as well as my biological son the same year. Eventually my wife and I would conceive our daughter. I was still drinking my life away, at this time which led me down a dark road of homelessness, incarceration and being a straight alcoholic.. This part of my life is when I became an addict.

Chapter 3:

Coming to grips that I've become an addict was a hard pill to swallow. So by the age of 24, I wound up having my last child, this one is with my wife. At this time, I remember like it was yesterday, my wife was telling me for years that if you have a drinking problem, you need to stop. I was so in denial because I'm thinking, **"Man, I'm not one of those people that go to meetings that need to raise his hand, and confess to being an addict."** You know, all that stuff I thought was for losers. But after coming to terms with myself, after many blackouts, and drunk fights, in which I will explain to you shortly, I finally said, **"Okay, I'm going to surrender. Well, at least attempt to and that's when the war began."** See, many of us don't understand the minute you surrender doesn't mean that you're gonna just stop, it just lets you know, **"Okay, that you have to fight in the war that is just beginning."** And I tell you, the war was hard for me. That's why I call my program **"Soldiers for Recovery,"** because you really have to be a soldier for your recovery. So I have to acknowledge that I'm an alcoholic. I went to my first

AA meeting up in Chestnut Hill, part of Philadelphia where it's nicer. And early on, you know, I started raising my hand speaking, but it didn't stop me from drinking. I still kept drinking. I couldn't find a way to stop, which later on led me to not coming home, drunk and blackouts, drunken fights. I remember waking up down Center City at the waterfront by the sound of lightning. When I went down there, I figured, I'll buy myself a bottle of Bacardi, and I'll sit by the water. Wow, great idea. Eventually I passed out from the Bacardi and awakened to the sound of lightning. When I went to sleep, it was daytime, I woke up at nighttime, and it was pouring down rain. Went in my pocket, no money, looked down at my feet, no sneakers. And I don't remember how I got there. But I do remember being there. But I still don't remember how I got there. And what I mean by getting there is, how did I get in this position? So I had to walk to the train station, from Delaware Avenue all the way to the regional rail at 15th & Market St. When I arrived I had to beg the train conductor to let me on. He knew me from catching the train because I used to always go to work from Chestnut Hill from that stop. While making my way home, my wife was there to help me. But that's just one of many episodes while battling addiction.

Here is yet another episode I remember where I went to this club close to my home. And I don't even remember everything that night. But what I do remember is this guy hit me in my head with a gun and split my head, as they say to the white meat, flesh, walking all the way home again and my wife had to patch me up. There were many nights and many days that I didn't come home and those nights and days I wouldn't even remember, I couldn't even tell you guys. but what I do know is that when I got paid, and I'm a barber, so I got paid every day. Friday was always dreadful for myself and my family because there was no telling if I was going to come home or even make it home safely. So after years and years of me surrendering. By the age of 29, I finally got into a fight with my sister's boyfriend after blacking out again arguing with my sister. And then I got hit in the head again and this time this one was bad. The next morning I woke up and what I realized is that I had a gash in the back of my head and was bleeding. So I called the ambulance, got rushed to the hospital to find out I had a concussion and bleeding on the brain which led me to stay in the hospital for a couple days. After that, upon my release, they gave me Percocet. And this is how I got introduced to taking opiods. This is how I became addicted to heroin. So as the doctor says, **"Okay, take these as prescribed,"** I was instructed to take 5 milligrams every four to six hours. I remember it like it was yesterday. In the beginning I took them as prescribed. Plus, it kind of forced me to stop drinking. Because I didn't want to kill myself. I never wanted to kill myself. And most addicts you see on the streets today, never plan on killing themselves. But what I realized is that while I was taking these opioids, I didn't have the desire to drink. Because I started feeling good with the Percocet. I love how it made me feel. I loved the fact that I didn't have to black out and also love the fact that I can go home every night. And I didn't have to spend a lot of money at that time.

So I said, **"Man, maybe I stopped drinking."** And guess what? I did. I stopped drinking, but I started consuming more and more Percocet. Eventually, what I realized that a lot of my clients were not just on Percocet, but they were also on harder drugs known as Oxycotton which was a more powerful opioid. Eventually, I started taking more and more Percocet until they couldn't help me get higher. After about a year of taking just regular Percocet, I began consuming about 60 pills a day eventually getting graduation papers to Oxys. I started taking 5 oxy 10

s eventually graduating to oxy 30s and doing nine of those a day. Then I learned about the Oxy 80s. So I wind up taking two Oxy 80s in the morning, two Oxy 80s in the afternoon, two Oxy 80s around three o'clock, and two more before bed. I wind up consuming eight Oxy 80s a day. And then here I go again, once again, broke, no money, watching my wife struggle to pay all the bills for so many years. Then one day, it was this guy who used to come in the shop to get his haircut. And he would ask me "Am I okay?", because he knew what I was doing but that was his way of introducing me to heroin. He came in one day and asked, . ***"Hey, man, you should try some of this heroin because you are spending too much money."*** And so for a couple of years, I'm like, ***"Nah, I'm not*** *trying heroin."* I'm about 30 years old at this time and I was using Percocet and Oxycodone for three years straight. Then one day my pill connection wasn't around. And he wound up coming to the shop on this day. I remember like it was yesterday I was going through withdrawal. I'm shaking and I'm sweating. He said, *"You look like you're going through it. Oh, buddy, I got some for that."* And he continues, *"You know what I got for you."* And I said, *"No".* But under that same breath of me saying *"No"*. I said, *"Hey man, let's talk outside."* We went outside. I said, *"Listen, man, I ain't doing needles because I don't do needles"*. He said, *"You don't need to do needles, all you need to do is sniff half of the bag."* So I took that bag, went in the bathroom, and I sniffed half the bag and there was my introduction to heroin. So after consuming that bag, I wound up traveling to Kensington, Philadelphia and getting more and more for many years which led me down a road of homelessness. I wound up being homeless three times with my family due to the disease of addiction. I found myself living in Kensington many nights sleeping on the streets taking heroin. And I always thought that it couldn't be me. Look at me now.

Sleeping on the streets, eating on the streets, going barefoot while my family had to survive whichever way they could.

Chapter 4:

So after using heroin, my whole life changed. It led me on a very, very dark journey. Nothing mattered to me then, just getting high. And I became a terrible barber in between. Like, I thought I was a great barber before, but the drugs made me worse.. I remember leaving my clients in the chair for 45 minutes or more. Clients would come and they knew I had to get my fix. So I will ask them for $20 for the hair cut, which I haven't done yet. And also the keys to their car. And can you believe that they will actually give me their car. See, I always was a good person, even during my time of drug use, but I wasn't good to my family. But at least to my clients, because I knew they had the money. So overall, I was a good person outside of drugs and alcohol. My clients knew that they could trust me with a car because all I'm going to do is go get the drugs and come right back. Use them and give them the best cut of their life. But deep down inside, I was crying. Deep down inside, I was hurting. The emptiness of growing up without a dad, the emptiness of growing up with mom being on drugs and father being absent. My stepfather being an addict, being bullied, being pushed around as a young man. But then as I got older, it turned into me selling drugs and drinking and street wars with people not being pushed around anymore, but just being respected led to me being an addict. My natural weight was 170 as an adult. I was 110 - 115 pounds due to the disease of addiction. I never imagined in my wildest dreams my life would be this way. Waking up at night, just to get high and being content and complacent where I was. Wearing the same clothes, not bathing, not washing, not brushing my teeth, I didn't even care about food. I've attempted to get clean a couple times throughout this experience. You know, I went in and out of detox centers at least 1000 times. I relapsed like a million times.

After being homeless for some time from substance abuse, eventually my wife and I got our home back. I was still using and started getting tired and started getting honest with myself. I got tired of saying, **"Oh God, I won't do it again. I won't do it again."** But when I got honest with God I said this prayer. I will never forget it. I got down on my knees and I said, **"God, I'm not going to stop using but I dont want to kill myself. And I encourage you guys to use what I'm saying right now."** I got honest with God. I said, **"God, I'm not going to stop using,"** there weren't any more crocodile tears saying **"Oh, God, this my last time, it wasn't none of that. This time it was different. It felt different."** I said, **"God, I'm not going to stop using. I'm going to keep using. I'm going to keep drinking. I'm going to keep smoking cigarettes. I'm going to keep doing what I was doing, living a reckless and dangerous lifestyle until I kill myself. Not intentionally, but until the addiction kills me."** But I say, **"God, if you got something good for me, like if it's something I'm supposed to be doing good, if I have a purpose in life, if I got a chance to make it to Heaven, can you please move this disease of addiction from me?** And that was it. I continued on using it for three months straight. Then one day I woke up out of bed as I prepare myself to go get drugs and go to work. Something told me not today. I've turned over to my wife. I said, **"Baby I'm going into rehab"**. She said, **"What? I thought you stopped."** I said, **"I never stopped. I'm going into rehab."** This was the best decision I ever made in my life. I never picked up another drug or drink again.. I sit here today with ten years clean free from the disease of addiction. See, it ain't happening until I got honest. God removed that burning desire for me to use. See, a lot of you guys got to be honest about yourself situation. And what I mean by that, and what does that look like when I say that, **"You have to be honest with God. And if you ain't going to stop using, then just be honest."**

Today, I sit here ten years clean after I got out of that rehab, which was about 30 days. They told me I couldn't come back for 30 days to start speaking. I went back up there the following Sunday and started and to my surprise they let me speak and I've been sharing my story ever since. And then when

COVID-19 came, I changed my pivot and started what you all know today as *"Soldiers for Recovery"*. *"Soldiers for Recovery"* started as a message every day on Instagram, to influence those who suffer substance abuse disorder to get help. It started off with one follower, but today, it's 1000s. *"Soldiers for Recovery"* has influenced many people throughout the world to find sobriety. *"Soldiers for Recovery"* started in my hometown of Philadelphia, where it now has reached a worldwide audience. My sobriety has influenced so many people to get clean with my life story. My story has helped so many people want to find recovery and learn to live a more fulfilling and healthier lifestyle. I didn't know what I was building or working on. Today *"Soldiers for Recovery"* has its own program. It's called the *"No Man Left Behind"* program which helps those who not only struggle with the disease of addiction, but struggling with any kind of addiction. Now, how did I get here? I got here by surrendering. And how can this help you? It can help you by doing the same thing that I did. Because when I went into that rehab broken, I came out and got to the core of my disease and why I kept losing which was trauma, which many of us suffer and go through. So throughout this book, I'm going to have a few points and a few tips that you can use like me, in order to give your life over to a higher power greater than yourself. So you can become a soldier for your recovery as well. I appreciate your time. Thank you.

Conclusion

Moving Forward: Staying Clean and Finding Support

As we near the end of our journey through this book, it's important to remember that recovery is an ongoing process. It doesn't end here; rather, this is where another chapter of your life begins. A life where you are in control, aware of your strengths, and equipped to face challenges. Let's talk about how to maintain the progress you've made and continue to thrive in your sobriety.

Section 1: Tips for Staying Clean

Develop a Routine: Establishing a daily routine is vital in recovery. It provides structure and reduces the unpredictability that can lead to stress and relapse. Your routine should include time for work, rest, hobbies, and self-care. Remember, a well-organized day keeps negative thoughts and triggers at bay.

Stay Connected with Support Groups: The journey of recovery is not meant to be walked alone. Regular attendance at support group meetings, whether they're in your local community or online, can provide a sense of belonging and understanding. These groups offer a platform to share experiences, learn from others, and receive encouragement.

Practice Mindfulness and Self-Care: Mindfulness can help you stay grounded and centered, particularly during challenging times. Techniques like meditation, deep breathing, and yoga can enhance your mental clarity and emotional balance. Alongside these practices, ensure you're engaging in activities that nurture your body and soul, be it reading, walking in nature, or pursuing a hobby.

Avoid Risky Situations: Be proactive in recognizing situations or people that may trigger a relapse. This might mean changing your social circles or avoiding certain places. Remember, it's not just about resisting temptation, but also about creating an environment that supports your sobriety.

Section 2: Resources for Addiction

List of Helpful Websites and Hotlines: Here's a list of resources where you can seek help anytime:

- National Helpline
- Alcoholics Anonymous
- Narcotics Anonymous

For immediate assistance, don't hesitate to call a local hotline or emergency number.

Recommended Reading: Enhance your understanding and coping strategies with books like "The Recovery Book" by Al J. Mooney M.D., and "Clean: Overcoming Addiction and Ending America's Greatest Tragedy" by David Sheff.

Local and Online Support Groups: Seek out local community centers or online platforms that host support group meetings. Websites like Meetup can be useful for finding local groups.

Outreach Programs: Many communities have outreach programs for addiction recovery. These can be great platforms for you to contribute and make a difference. Check with local health services or community centers for opportunities.

How You Can Become a Soldier in the Battle for Recovery

Becoming a soldier in the battle for recovery means standing strong beside those who are fighting their way back from addiction. It requires empathy, resilience, and a commitment to supporting your loved one through every victory and setback. As an ally, your role is not just to offer encouragement but to equip yourself with the knowledge, resources, and tools needed to make a meaningful difference. In the following sections, you'll find practical tips, valuable resources, and reflective questions to guide you in becoming a steadfast supporter on this challenging but rewarding journey.

Reflection Questions

- What part of my story resonated most with you? Why?

_____
_____
_____
_____
_____
_____
_____
_____

- What challenges have you faced in your own life that you see parallels with? How did you handle them?

_____
_____
_____
_____

_____

_____

_____

_____

- In moments of struggle, where do you find your strength? How can you build on this source of strength?

_____

_____

_____

_____

_____

_____

_____

_____

_____

- What are some habits or patterns in your life that you feel need change? How will you begin to address them?

_____
_____
_____
_____
_____
_____
_____
_____
_____

True and False Questions

True or False: Recovery is a one-time event, not a lifelong journey.

True or False: Asking for help is a sign of weakness in the recovery process.

_____

True or False: Building a supportive community is essential to maintaining long-term recovery.

_____

True or False: Relapses are a normal part of recovery and should be accepted without guilt.

_____

Action Steps

- Write down three steps you can take this week to support your recovery or personal growth.

_____

_____

_____

_____

_____

_____

_____

- List three people you can reach out to for support or encouragement. How will you approach them?

_____

_____

_____

_____

_____

_____

_____

_____

_____

_____

- Identify one habit that you want to change. What is your plan to replace it with positive behavior?

_____
_____
_____
_____
_____
_____
_____
_____

Inspirational Quotes

- "The only way to deal with fear is to face it head-on."

- "Recovery is not about perfection; it's about progress.

Journaling Prompts

- Describe a time when you felt most empowered during your recovery journey. What can you learn from that experience?

_____
_____
_____
_____
_____
_____
_____
_____
_____
_____
_____
_____
_____

- What does freedom from addiction look like to you? How can you visualize this in your daily life?

_____

_____

_____

_____

_____

_____

_____

_____

_____

_____

_____

Becoming an Ally: Support with Compassion and Understanding

Understanding Addiction

* Addiction is a Disease: Addiction is a chronic illness, not a moral failing.

* The Importance of Empathy: Empathy and patience are key in supporting someone battling addiction.

* Breaking the Stigma: Approach the situation without judgment and be aware of the stigma surrounding addiction.

Tips for Being an Effective Ally

- Educate Yourself: Learn about the nature of addiction, its causes, and the recovery process.

- Listen Without Judgment: Sometimes, just listening without offering solutions can be the most supportive action.

- Set Boundaries: Take care of your own well-being while supporting someone else. Understand that you cannot "fix" them.

- Encourage Professional Help: Offer to help them find a therapist, attend meetings, or explore treatment options.

- Be Patient and Persistent: Recovery is a long journey, and your support can make a big difference even if progress is slow.

Conclusion

You've made it through this book, but more importantly, you've made significant strides in your journey to recovery. Remember, every day is a new opportunity to reinforce your commitment to a clean and fulfilling life. You are not alone in this journey; there's a world of support out there. Stay strong, stay connected, and continue to nurture the beautiful life you are rebuilding.

About the Author

Founder and CEO of Soldiers For Recovery Inc., Suleiman Hassan, has dedicated his life to supporting the vulnerable populations in Philadelphia. For many years, he shared his talents and expertise of motivational speaking by providing consultation to the Substance Abuse population.

Through his personal experiences, Suleiman wants to ensure that people with addiction problems can find their inner voice and have access and empowerment to recovery.

Suleiman is an official member for the Alcoholism and Drug Abuse Counselors, as well as a certified Forensic Addictions Peer Specialist.

Answer Key: True or False Questions

1. **True or False: Recovery is a one-time event, not a lifelong journey.**
   Answer: False. Recovery is an ongoing process that requires continuous effort and commitment.
2. **True or False: Asking for help is a sign of weakness in the recovery process.**
   Answer: False. Asking for help is a sign of strength and an important step in recovery.
3. **True or False: Building a supportive community is essential to maintaining long-term recovery.**
   Answer: True. A supportive network can provide encouragement, accountability, and strength.
4. **True or False: Relapses are a normal part of recovery and should be accepted without guilt.**
   Answer: True. Relapses can happen, and it's important to learn from them without self-judgment.

Made in the USA
Middletown, DE
29 September 2024